BUTTERFLIES
and other insects

Sally Morgan

Belitha Press

First published in the UK in 2001 by

Belitha Press Limited, London House,
Great Eastern Wharf, Parkgate Road,
London SW11 4NQ

Copyright © Belitha Press Limited 2001
Text by Sally Morgan

Includes specialist photography by Robert Pickett

Series editor: Russell McLean
Editor: Jinny Johnson
Designer: Jacqueline Palmer
Educational consultant: Emma Harvey,
    Honeywell Infants School, London

ISBN 1 84138 310 4

Printed in Hong Kong

British Library Cataloguing in Publication Data
for this book is available from the British Library.

10 9 8 7 6 5 4 3 2 1

Picture acknowledgements:
JAL Cooke/OSF: 8t, 29tr. Stephen Dalton/NHPA: front cover c, 20t, 29c.
Papilio: 5t, 7b, 11t, 13b, 24bl, 24br, 25cl, 25cr, 25b, 27br, 28t, 28b. Dr Eckart
Pott/NHPA: 21l. Ken Preston-Mafham/Premaphotos: front cover t, 5b, 7t, 9c,
11br, 13t, 13c, 19tr, 19b, 22bl, 23tr, 23bl, 24t, 26t, 26b, 27tr. Mark Preston-
Mafham/Premaphotos: 19tl, 21tr. Kjell Sandved/Ecoscene: 22tl, 27tl.
Kim Taylor/Bruce Coleman Ltd: 15b. Ken Wilson/Papilio/Corbis: 21b.

All other photographs by Robert Pickett

While every attempt has been made to clear copyrights, should there
be inadvertent omissions please apply to the publisher for rectification.

Contents

The butterfly in this book is a monarch, which lives in the Americas and may visit Europe in late summer. Panels at the top of the pages show when each stage in the butterfly's life cycle takes place. The sections on a yellow background give information about the life cycles of other insects as well as other butterfly species.

Words in **bold** are explained in the glossary on page 30.

Time panel

Information about other insects and butterfly species

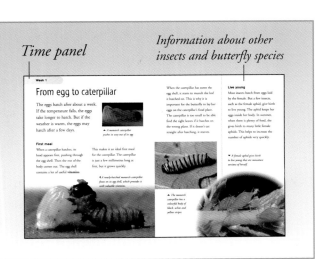

What is a butterfly?

A butterfly is a type of **insect** with colourful, shimmering wings. Its body is made up of three parts – a head, a **thorax** and an **abdomen**. Three pairs of legs and two pairs of wings are attached to the thorax. On the head are two **compound eyes** and a pair of **antennae**, or feelers.

◀ *You can easily tell a monarch butterfly by its striking wings, which are black and orange with white spots around the edges.*

Butterflies are found all over the world – anywhere where plants grow. There are at least 150 000 different **species** of butterflies and moths. The largest, most colourful butterflies live in the **tropics**, especially in tropical rainforests.

Changing shape

The life cycle of a butterfly has four stages – egg, **larva** or **caterpillar**, **pupa** and adult. A caterpillar looks nothing like an adult. The change from a caterpillar to an adult is called **metamorphosis**. This means 'change in body shape'.

▲ *Birdwing butterflies, such as this green birdwing, are among the largest and most colourful of all butterflies. They live in the forests of Southeast Asia and Australia.*

▼ *A red daggerwing caterpillar crawls over a leaf.*

Laying eggs

The life cycle of a monarch butterfly begins in late spring and early summer when the adults **mate**. Then the female lays her eggs.

▲ *The egg of a monarch butterfly is just a few millimetres long.*

The female has to lay her eggs on a plant that her caterpillars like to eat. This is called the food plant. The monarch butterfly lays her eggs on the milkweed plant. If she picks the wrong plant, the caterpillars will starve.

Protective shells

Each egg has a hard shell which protects the developing young inside. The monarch's egg has tiny ridges on its surface. Only one in every 100 eggs survives and hatches. Many are eaten by birds and insects, while others are killed by disease.

◀ *A female monarch butterfly lays her eggs on the leaf of a milkweed plant.*

6

All sorts of eggs

Each type of insect has eggs of a certain colour and shape. Most insects lay their eggs in particular places. The tortoiseshell butterfly lays her yellow-coloured eggs in piles of about 20. She may lay as many as 1000 eggs over a few days. Some moths lay their eggs in a long chain wrapped around a small twig. The potter wasp makes a nest like a small pot of clay in which she lays a single egg. Green lacewings lay eggs that are supported on long stalks. This helps to keep the eggs out of reach of **predators**.

▲ *The potter wasp lays an egg in her clay nest. She adds a caterpillar for her young to eat when it hatches.*

▼ *The green lacewing attaches each of her eggs to a long, sticky thread which comes from her abdomen. The thread hardens to make a stalk.*

From egg to caterpillar

The eggs hatch after about a week. If the temperature falls, the eggs take longer to hatch. But if the weather is warm, the eggs may hatch after a few days.

▲ *A monarch caterpillar pushes its way out of its egg.*

First meal

When a caterpillar hatches, its head appears first, pushing through the egg shell. Then the rest of the body comes out. The egg shell contains a lot of useful **vitamins**.

This makes it an ideal first meal for the caterpillar. The caterpillar is just a few millimetres long at first, but it grows quickly.

◀ *A newly-hatched monarch caterpillar feasts on its egg shell, which provides it with valuable vitamins.*

When the caterpillar has eaten the egg shell, it starts to munch the leaf it hatched on. This is why it is important for the butterfly to lay her eggs on the caterpillar's food plant. The caterpillar is too small to be able find the right leaves if it hatches on the wrong plant. If it doesn't eat straight after hatching, it starves.

Live young

Most insects hatch from eggs laid by the female. But a few insects, such as the female aphid, give birth to live young. The aphid keeps her eggs inside her body. In summer, when there is plenty of food, she gives birth to many little female aphids. This helps to increase the number of aphids very quickly.

▼ *A female aphid gives birth to live young that are miniature versions of herself.*

▲ *The monarch caterpillar has a colourful body of black, white and yellow stripes.*

Growing quickly

The caterpillar looks nothing like the adult butterfly. In fact, the two look so different that you can't tell they are the same type of insect.

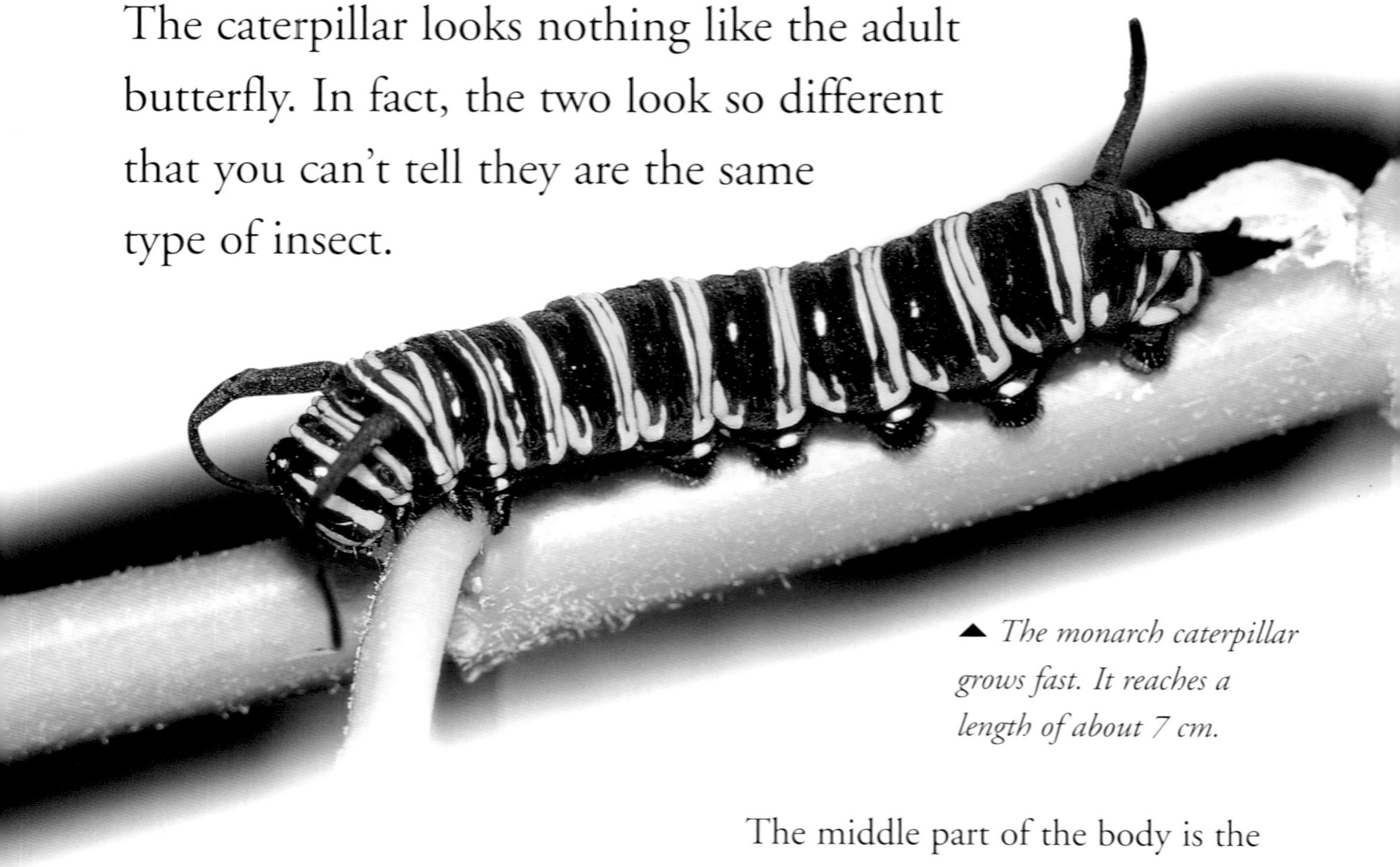

▲ *The monarch caterpillar grows fast. It reaches a length of about 7 cm.*

Body parts

The caterpillar's body is made up of many segments, or parts. On its head (on the left of the picture above) are six simple eyes arranged in a horseshoe pattern and a pair of short antennae. The caterpillar has strong jaws with teeth that can rip through leaves.

The middle part of the body is the thorax, which has three segments. A pair of **jointed** legs is attached to each segment. The rest of the body is made up of the abdomen. Attached to the abdomen are four pairs of soft, muscular **prolegs.** Along the side of the body are tiny holes called **spiracles** which are used for breathing.

10

Eat, eat, eat

The caterpillar has a huge appetite. It eats all day, chewing through lots of milkweed leaves. Each day, the caterpillar grows larger. The skin of the caterpillar does not stretch much, so the caterpillar has to **moult**. This means that it sheds its old skin to reveal a new soft skin, which will stretch before it dries and hardens.

Puss moth caterpillar

False legs

The fleshy prolegs attached to the segments of a caterpillar's abdomen are not real legs, but they are still used for gripping stems and leaves. The prolegs disappear when the caterpillar changes into an adult butterfly.

▲▼ *A caterpillar's prolegs (top) are fleshy and end in* **suckers**. *The true legs are more pointed and end in claws (below).*

▲ *During the larval stage, the monarch caterpillar increases its length by up to 20 times, and its weight by thousands of times.*

Hawkmoth caterpillar

Self-defence

Only a few caterpillars survive life as a larva. Just like the eggs, only one in every 100 becomes a pupa. Caterpillars are a favourite food of many birds and other animals, and others die of disease. Many caterpillars have ways of defending themselves from their predators.

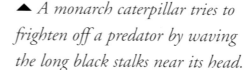

▲ *A monarch caterpillar tries to frighten off a predator by waving the long black stalks near its head.*

Warning signs

Many caterpillars, including monarch caterpillars, are **poisonous**. Their food plant, the milkweed, is poisonous, so when the caterpillars eat the leaves, they become poisonous too. The yellow, black and white markings on the caterpillar warn birds that it tastes nasty and may be harmful.

Scare tactics

Some caterpillars try to scare away predators. The monarch caterpillar has two long, black filaments, or stalks, at each end of its body. It waves these to put off birds.

Some caterpillars, such as the puss moth, rear up and try to look larger than they really are. Other caterpillars are covered in stinging hairs which irritate the skin of a predator.

Camouflage

Many caterpillars protect themselves by hiding from their predators. Some are **camouflaged** – coloured so that they blend with their background. The shape of their body may look like an old leaf or the end of a twig. When these caterpillars lie still they are almost impossible to spot. They move slowly so as not to draw attention to themselves.

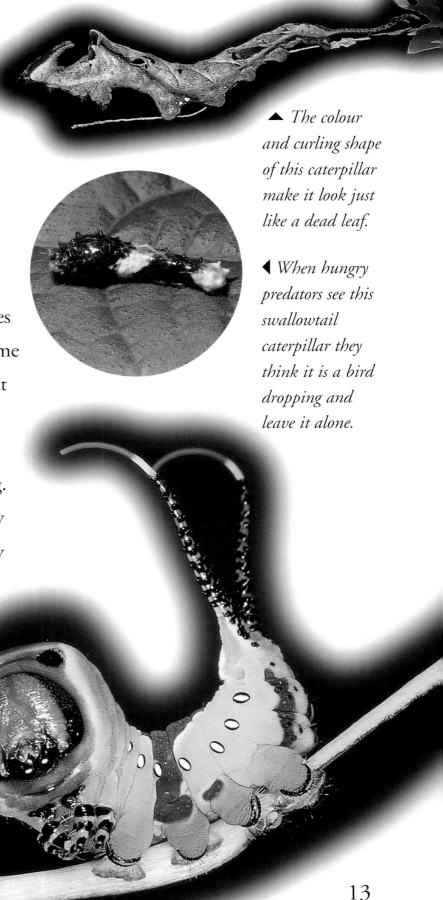

▲ *The colour and curling shape of this caterpillar make it look just like a dead leaf.*

◀ *When hungry predators see this swallowtail caterpillar they think it is a bird dropping and leave it alone.*

▶ *A puss moth caterpillar rears up both the back and front of its body to scare off an enemy. It can also squirt a stinging liquid at its attacker.*

13

Time for change

When the caterpillar reaches its full size, it stops feeding. It goes through its last moult and becomes a pupa. Then it enters the transformation stage, when it changes from a caterpillar to an adult butterfly.

▲ *This monarch caterpillar attaches itself to the underside of a leaf and prepares to pupate.*

A safe place

First, the caterpillar has to find a safe place to **pupate**. Some butterflies hang under leaves or seek shelter under roofs or in sheds.

▲ *The pupal case is beginning to form around this monarch caterpillar.*

▲ *The pupal case is complete. Inside, the caterpillar begins to change into a butterfly.*

During the pupal stage, the pupal case changes colour. It turns a bluish-green with metallic gold spots.

Monarchs choose to hang from the stems and leaf stalks of their food plant, the milkweed. The caterpillar attaches its suckers to a small pad of silk which it spins on the stalk. This keeps the caterpillar secure while it pupates. Its skin hardens and turns into a pupal case. From the outside it may look like not much is happening, but big changes are taking place inside the pupa. The body of the caterpillar is being broken down and rearranged into the shape of an adult butterfly.

Spinning a cocoon

Some caterpillars make a **cocoon** in which they pupate. The cocoon is made from silk threads which the caterpillar pushes out from its abdomen. The silk moth caterpillar spins a cocoon in this way. In silk making, the silk thread is unwound, washed, dyed and used to make silk cloth. Other caterpillars wrap a leaf around themselves and use silk to hold the leaf edges together.

▼ *The silk moth caterpillar spins a cocoon of silk in which to pupate.*

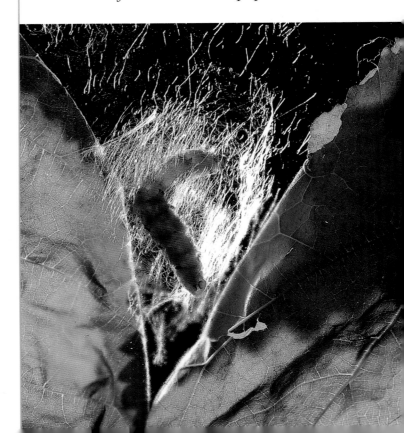

A new butterfly

Once the changes have taken place inside the pupa, the adult butterfly is ready to come out. Towards the end of pupation, movements can be seen inside the pupal case. Finally, the pupa splits open and the new adult pushes out.

▲ *The pupal case is beginning to split.*

▲ *The new adult butterfly comes out of the pupal case.*

▲ *The butterfly rests for a moment outside the pupa.*

At first, the monarch butterfly's wings are soft, wrinkled and pale. It may take a couple of hours for the wings to open up and stiffen and for the full colour to develop. Then the butterfly is ready to fly away and begin its adult life.

Drying wings

This is a critical stage for the new butterfly. Its body is damp and its wings are crumpled. It has to stretch out and dry its wings before it can fly. First, it crawls to a place where it can hang by its legs and let its wings dangle.

Then it pumps blood into the veins which run through its wings, and the wings open out to full size. This takes about 20 minutes. But it may take two hours for the wings to become stiff enough for the butterfly to fly away.

Finding food

Some butterflies only live a few days and do not need to feed. They come out of their pupal cases, find a mate and lay their eggs. Others live for longer, so they need to find food.

Liquid feeders

Butterflies such as the monarch feed on liquid foods. These include the sugary **nectar** made by flowers, and the juice of fruits. A butterfly has a long, hollow feeding tube called a **proboscis,** which it uses to suck up liquid food. The monarch butterfly settles on a flower, plunges its proboscis into the bloom and sucks the nectar through the tube. When the proboscis is not being used, it is coiled up in a spiral under the head.

▲ *A monarch lands on a flower to feed on the rich, sugary nectar it contains.*

▲ *The proboscis is held curled up in a spiral.*

▶ *The butterfly unfurls its proboscis and starts to feed.*

18

▲ *A large ground beetle attacks a smaller tenebrionid beetle.*

▶ *A grasshopper uses its strong jaws to munch leaves.*

Plant eaters and hunters

The diets of other insects are very varied. Aphids and many bugs feed on liquids just like butterflies, but they have mouthparts which can pierce plant stems too. They suck liquid out of the plant. Like caterpillars, grasshoppers and locusts have strong jaws to chew tough leaves.

The earwig is a harmless plant eater, or **herbivore**, that likes to eat flowering plants. Many insects are **carnivores** which hunt other animals. Dragonflies, ladybirds and ground beetles are all hunters.

◀ *The stinkbug pierces a plant stem with its strong mouthparts.*

Surviving winter

Butterflies need warm weather. If the temperature falls, so does the temperature of their body. If they become too cold, they cannot fly. Many butterflies spend the winter in hiding places that keep them safe and dry until spring arrives.

◀ *The monarch can fly as far as 130 km in a day.*

Long flight

The monarch butterfly spends the summer in the central states of the United States and in Canada. In autumn, the butterflies fly south to spend the winter in California and Mexico. Here, they gather in large numbers and come to rest on trees known as **roosts**. They spend most of the winter sleeping.

In spring, the longer days and the warmer temperatures wake up the butterflies and they begin their long journey north. They mate and lay their eggs on the way. These butterflies will not make the return journey south. The ones that return are the butterflies that hatch during the summer months.

▶ *Millions of monarchs spend the winter in the same trees year after year.*

20

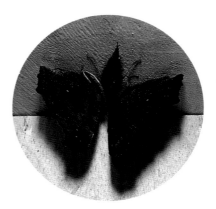

◀ *This peacock butterfly is hibernating in the roof of a shed.*

Other survivors

Peacock butterflies spend the winter **hibernating** in sheds and greenhouses. Other types of butterfly survive the winter as either eggs, caterpillars or pupae. The eggs of the chalk hill blue are laid in late summer, but do not hatch until the following April. The caterpillars of the silver-washed fritillary hibernate in trees and emerge in spring when they start eating again. Some pupae can survive for many years, waiting for the right conditions before the adult emerges.

▶ *After hibernation, the silver-washed fritillary caterpillar feeds on violet leaves.*

Finding a mate

Most of the time, butterflies live a **solitary** life, but they have to be able to find a mate.

Smells in the air

Female butterflies release chemicals called **pheromones** into the air. Male monarch butterflies have an excellent sense of smell. They can detect the pheromones even if they are several kilometres from the female. They fly towards the source of the smell.

◀ *A male and female monarch butterfly rest on a flower as they mate.*

Moths

Moths have an even better sense of smell, helped by their large feathery antennae (left). Their sense of smell is so good that they can detect places on the ground where a female moth rested.

Mating dances

Sometimes, when male and female butterflies meet, they do a mating dance. This may involve spiralling up into the air together or flashing their wings at each other.

▲ *A grasshopper perches on a leaf to begin his mating song.*

▲ *In the Amazon rainforest, a male heliconid butterfly performs a hovering mating dance above the female he is trying to attract.*

Sound and colour

A male grasshopper uses sound to attract females. First he chirps and when a female approaches him, he performs a mating song by rubbing a ridged area on his back leg against the side of the front wing.

Glow-worms use colour to attract a mate. At night, a female climbs to the top of a plant and points her abdomen into the air. She produces an eerie yellow light from the base of her abdomen. Males have much better eyesight than the females and can see her light from more than 10m away.

23

Other life cycles

A butterfly goes through four stages in its life cycle. Many insects pass through only three stages – egg, larva and adult. This is called incomplete metamorphosis because there is no pupal stage.

▲ *A female dragonfly lays her eggs on rushes floating on the surface of a pond.*

Dragonflies, aphids, grasshoppers and locusts all go through incomplete metamorphosis. Their larvae look similar to adults, but they are much smaller and do not have any wings.

The larvae go through a series of moults, often as many as 15, growing larger each time. After the final moult the adult is revealed, complete with a set of wings.

▼ *A dragonfly larva is called a nymph and lives in water.*

▲ *When it is ready for its final moult, the nymph crawls out of the water.*

Dragonfly nymphs

The dragonfly lays her eggs on the leaves of water plants in ponds, lakes and rivers. The eggs hatch into small larvae called **nymphs.** These live in the water for as long as three years, catching **prey** such as tadpoles and gradually growing larger. When they are ready to go through their last moult and change into adults, they crawl out of the water on to plant stems. Then they split their skin and a winged adult emerges.

Grasshopper young

Grasshoppers usually lay their eggs on the ground. The eggs hatch into larvae called nymphs which look like tiny versions of their parents. The nymphs cannot fly and are a different colour from adults. It may take the nymphs two months to grow wings. During this time they eat, grow and go through five or six moults. With each moult, their wings grow bigger. After their final moult, their wings are fully formed.

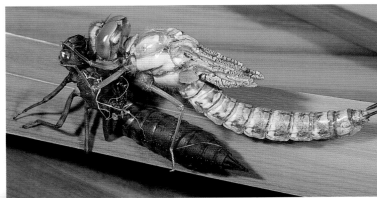

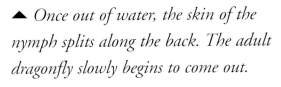

▲ *Once out of water, the skin of the nymph splits along the back. The adult dragonfly slowly begins to come out.*

▶ *The dragonfly must wait until its wings have dried and strengthened before flying away.*

All sorts of insects

There are more insects than any other type of animal. Insects can survive in some of the most difficult places on Earth. They are found living everywhere from the tropics to the poles, in water, on land and in the air.

▲ *A bumblebee fills its **pollen** sacs with pollen from a flower.*

One reason for the success of insects is the speed at which they multiply. Female insects lay hundreds of eggs. A queen termite can lay more than 30 000 eggs each day.

More than a million

Nobody is sure how many different species of insect there are. At least a million are already known and another 10 000 new types are discovered each year.

Beetles are the biggest group of insects. More than 250 000 different species are known so far. Beetles have thick, hard front wings which cover and protect the more delicate back wings.

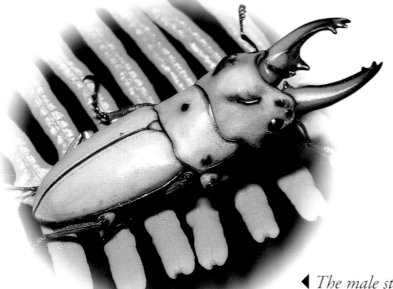

◀ *The male stag beetle has large jaws.*

Many insects are called flies, but true flies have just one pair of wings. Instead of a second pair, they have small knobbed stalks called halteres. These help the fly balance in the air.

▲ *A fly has compound eyes made up of many mini-eyes, each with its own tiny lens.*

Grasshoppers and crickets are insects with an extra-long pair of back legs which they use for jumping and making mating calls. Some can leap 200 times their own length. Grasshoppers have shorter antennae than crickets. Crickets have a flatter body and a pair of 'tails' that stick out from the end of the abdomen (right).

▶ *This bush cricket is ready to leap with the help of its long back legs.*

▶ *Leaf-cutter ants carry a leaf to their nest.*

Ants, bees and wasps all belong to the same large group of insects. They have a narrow waist between their thorax and abdomen. Bees and wasps have two pairs of wings, while ants are usually wingless.

People often call insects bugs. But a true bug is a small animal with stabbing mouthparts which can suck liquid from plants or animals.

Amazing insects

- The biggest insect that ever lived was a dragonfly. It lived 310 million years ago and had a wingspan of 70 cm. That's probably longer than your arm. The largest living dragonfly has a wingspan of less than 13 cm.

- The longest insect is a tropical stick insect from the rainforests of Borneo. Its legs stick out in front of and behind its body to make a total length of more than 50 cm.

- The fastest insect is the cockroach (below) which moves at more than 4 km an hour.

- The Atlas moth (above) has the largest wingspan of any insect. Its wings measure 30 cm from tip to tip.

- The largest living insect is the goliath beetle which weighs in at 100g. It is 10 cm long and is almost the size of a computer mouse.

- The smallest insect is the fairy fly, which is just one quarter of a millimetre long and could fly through the eye of a needle!

- The wings of the swallowtail butterfly beat 300 times per minute. But midges can beat their wings an amazing 1000 times per second. This makes the high-pitched whine you hear when mosquitoes and midges are around.

The life cycle of a butterfly

1 *The eggs of the monarch butterfly are laid on a leaf.*

8 *In spring and early summer, the butterfly finds a mate and the female lays her eggs.*

2 *About a week later, a caterpillar hatches out of the egg.*

3 *The caterpillar feeds on leaves and grows quickly.*

7 *The adult butterfly feeds on nectar.*

6 *When the changes are complete, the pupa splits and the adult butterfly comes out.*

4 *When the caterpillar reaches its full size it becomes a pupa.*

5 *Inside the pupa, the caterpillar's body is rearranged into the shape of an adult butterfly.*

29

Glossary

abdomen The third part of an insect's body, behind the head and thorax.

antenna (plural **antennae**) Slender structures on an insect's head that help it sense things in its surroundings. Antennae are often known as feelers.

camouflage The way in which the colour or body shape of an insect helps it to hide in its surroundings and protect itself from predators.

carnivore An animal that eats other animals.

caterpillar An early stage in the life of a butterfly, a caterpillar looks completely different from an adult butterfly. It spends its time feeding and growing.

cocoon A case of silk spun by a caterpillar in which to pupate.

compound eye An eye made up of lots of mini-eyes. Each mini-eye has its own tiny lens.

herbivore An animal that eats plants.

hibernate To spend the winter in a deep sleep.

insect An animal with six legs and a body made up of a head, thorax and abdomen. Many, but not all, insects also have two pairs of wings.

jointed Having joints – the places where two moving parts meet.

larva (plural **larvae**) The young form of an insect. A larva often looks very different from the adult insect.

mate To pair or breed.

metamorphosis A change in body shape or appearance – for example, when a caterpillar turns into an adult butterfly.

moult To shed an old skin to reveal a new, often larger, skin below.

nectar The sugary liquid produced by flowers. Many insects feed on nectar.

nymph The name given to the young of insects such as dragonflies.

pheromones Scented chemicals which some insects make in their bodies to help them attract mates.

poisonous Harmful.

pollen Yellow, powdery grains made by the male parts of a flower.

predator An animal that hunts and kills other animals for food.

prey Animals killed by others for food.

proboscis The feeding tube of an insect through which it sucks liquid food such as nectar.

proleg Fleshy, muscular structures attached to a caterpillar's abdomen that help it hold on to plants.

pupa (plural **pupae**) A stage in the life cycle of an insect during which it changes from a larva to an adult.

pupate To become a pupa.

roost A place such as a tree where an insect or other animal rests for the night.

solitary Living alone.

species A particular type of animal that can only breed with others of the same type. Each species is given a unique name. There are more species of insect than of any other animal.

spiracles Tiny holes along the sides of an insect's body which it uses to breathe.

sucker A pad which sticks firmly to the surface of something.

thorax The second part of an insect's body, between the head and the abdomen.

tropics The area on either side of the Equator, where it is warm and wet for all or most of the year.

vitamins Important nutrients in food which an animal needs for healthy growth.

Index